Struik Pocket Guides
for Southern Africa

Common Trees of Southern Africa

Eugene and Glen Moll

ILLUSTRATED BY

D1427954

STRUIK

Contents

Struik Publishers (Pty) Ltd
(a member of The Struik Publishing Group (Pty) Ltd)
Cornelis Struik House
80 McKenzie Street
Cape Town 8001

Reg. No.: 54/00965/07

First Published 1989
Second Impression 1992
Third Impression 1993
Second Edition 1994
Second Impression 1996

Setting by cmyk Prepress (Pty) Ltd, Cape Town
Reproduction by cmyk Prepress (Pty) Ltd, Cape Town
Printing and binding by CTP Book Printers, Parow

ISBN 1 86825 506 9

Front and back cover: Coast erythrina (*Erythrina caffra*)

Introduction

There are more than 1 500 indigenous tree species in southern Africa. Many of these are trees which we see every day. In wet regions trees can be very large and may occur in dense communities where their crowns touch or intermingle, while in more arid areas they are usually widely scattered and often short. Trees differ widely from area to area: they may be short and fat or tall and thin, the canopy may be widely spreading or dense, and the branches may bear flowers and fruit of various colours, shapes, sizes, scents, textures and tastes.

Arguments abound as to the exact definition of a tree. However, most agree that it is a woody plant of stature, usually several metres high and often with an unbranched stem (the trunk or bole) of a metre or more. Unlike many other plants, trees are readily identified by characters other than floral. Some, like palms and aloes, have a characteristic growth form, others have a unique stem (baobab) or bark (tamboti). The sausage tree and sickle bush have persistent fruits that make identification simple. Almost all trees, however, have a combination of leaf characteristics which facilitate identification, meaning that most trees can be recognized by vegetative rather than floral criteria.

Botanically, all trees are classified into plant families, based on floral characteristics. Plant families are then divided into genera (sing. genus), which in turn are divided into one or several species or specific kinds. Individual plants are given a specific botanical name – a binomial – made up of the genus and species names. For example, the most widespread tree in our area is *Acacia karroo*. The genus is *Acacia*, belonging to the family Fabaceae (formerly Leguminosae), and the specific name is *karroo*. Strict rules apply to scientific names and are accepted internationally. One such rule is that the original or oldest name assigned to an organism is the valid one: if a species is discovered and named, and then subsequently found to have been discovered and named at an earlier time, perhaps in another country, then the original name is the valid one. Thus scientific names may change as our knowledge grows.

The aim of this guide is to introduce more than 145 of southern Africa's most common and widespread trees. To help you identify these species, diagnostic features are emphasized in the colour illustrations and there is an easy-to-use key on the inside back cover.

NOTE: In the species section of the book:
• the botanical and common names are given for each species
• South African tree numbers are given after botanical names
• an * before a botanical name means that the tree is an alien species
• for ease of identification, trees have been grouped according to leaf morphology (form) rather than by families or genera
• some of the species described are very similar and share certain features; in such cases, the whole tree of **one** of the species is illustrated, while the leaves, and other diagnostic features, where relevant, are depicted for the other species. In such cases, the distributions of the similar species have been combined onto one map.

Protea nitida (86)
Wagon tree, Waboom

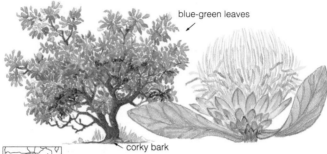

blue-green leaves

corky bark

Protea laurifolia (90,2)
Laurel protea, Louriersuikerbos

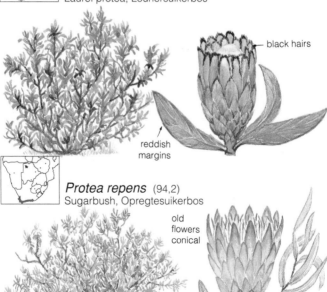

black hairs

reddish margins

Protea repens (94,2)
Sugarbush, Opregtesuikerbos

old flowers conical

Protea caffra (87)
Highveld protea, Hoëveldsuikerbos

Mostly seen as small old gnarled trees seldom exceeding 5 m; generally in groups on grassy mountain-sides and on dry rocky ridges. Bark rough and blackish; leaves pale green, sometimes blue-green, with little or no leafstalk. Whitish to pink flowers appear in summer from November to February.

Protea roupelliae (96)
Silver protea, Silwersuikerbos

A small tree usually with fewer branches than *P. caffra* and more upright, but seldom exceeding 6 m; also found in groups on grassy mountain-sides. Leaves often hairy and tend to stand upright at end of twigs. Flowers from August to April in a wide range of shades from pink to red.

Ficus spp.   *F. abutilifolia* (63) Large-leaved rock fig, Grootblaarrotsvy; *F. cordata* (51) Namaqua fig, Namakwavy; *F. stuhlmannii* (65) Lowveld fig, Laeveldvy; *F. ilicina* (53) Laurel fig, Louriervy

All fig species have a milky latex, and are best distinguished by size, type of fruit and whether the fruit grows on twigs or stems, and leaf shape. Stipules fall and leave conspicuous scars at base of leafstalk.

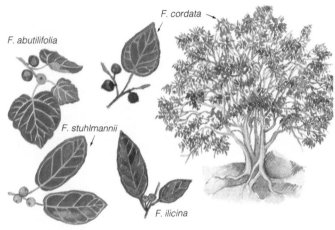

F. cordata

F. abutilifolia

F. stuhlmannii

F. ilicina

Ficus sycomorus (66)
Sycamore fig, Sycomorusvy

Commonly occurs along river banks as a large to extremely large fringing species with a strongly buttressed trunk. Bark typically yellow or greenish-yellow but may be pale brown. Leaves hairy and abrasive to the touch; fruit produced in large bunches on branches and stems.

Ficus spp. *F. ingens* (55) Red-leaved rock fig,
Rooiblaarrotsvy; *F. salicifolia* (60) Wonderboom fig,
Wonderboomvy; *F. lutea* (61) Giant-leaved fig,
Reuseblaarvy

F. ingens is often seen as a small tree clinging to bare rock. Leaves
usually pale green and thin, though young spring foliage spectacular
bronze. Both *F. salicifolia* and *F. lutea* are large, spreading trees, found
in kloofs and rocky areas, and in forest respectively.

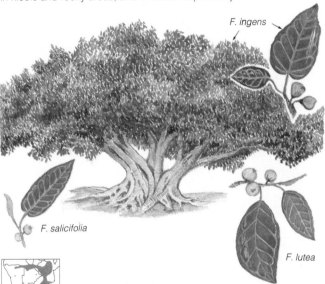

F. ingens

F. salicifolia

F. lutea

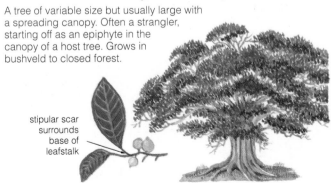

Ficus natalensis (57)
Common wild fig, Gewone wildevy

A tree of variable size but usually large with
a spreading canopy. Often a strangler,
starting off as an epiphyte in the
canopy of a host tree. Grows in
bushveld to closed forest.

stipular scar
surrounds
base of
leafstalk

Sideroxylon inerme (579)
White milkwood, Witmelkhout

This and the next three species belong to the family Sapotaceae. Characteristically, trees in this family contain milky latex in all parts.

A compact shrub or small tree up to 10 m, often occurring in coastal bush where it may form dense thickets; also in bushveld along the east coast. Leaves dark green and somewhat shiny above.

Bequaertiodendron magalismontanum (581)
Transvaal milkplum, Stamvrug

Usually a small tree up to 3 or 4 m and rarely 6-10 m, characteristic of rocky hillslopes. Foliage distinctive dark green above, golden-brown below. Flowers in spring; very tasty fruit borne on stems in summer. A close relative *B. natalense* (Natal milkplum, Natalmelkpruim: 582) is restricted to coastal forests in Transkei and Natal as a common understorey species.

golden-brown

Mimusops caffra (583)
Coast red-milkwood, Kusrooimelkhout

A small to medium-sized and occasionally a large tree up to 20 m, dominant in dune forests on sea-facing slopes. Leaves often bluish above, silvery below with curled-under margins. Whitish to cream flowers appear in spring, followed by fleshy, orange-red fruit in late summer. *M. obovata* (Red-milkwood, Rooimelkhout: 584), a closely related species with a rounded rather than truncated leaf apex, occurs in forests further inland.

Mimusops zeyheri (585)
Transvaal red-milkwood, Moepel

Usually a small to medium-sized tree less than 12 m high, found on rocky slopes in the lowveld or in riverine fringes. Bark dark and smooth, becoming rough with age. Canopy rounded; leaves thick and leathery; young twigs hairy. Flowers October to February; fruits April to July.

Faurea saligna (75)
Beechwood, Transvaalboekenhout

Usually a small tree 6-8 m high, occurring in small orchard-like groves on grassy, sandy hillslopes. Honey-scented flowers bloom in spring. A closely related species *F. galpinii* occurs at higher altitudes, and *F. speciosa* occurs in the north in mixed woodlands.

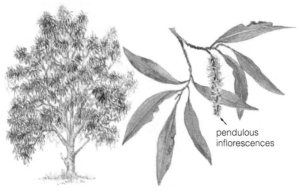

pendulous inflorescences

Podocarpus falcatus (16)
Outeniqua yellowwood, Outeniekwageelhout
Podocarpus latifolius (18)
Real yellowwood, Opregte geelhout

Both forest species with narrow leaves, *P. falcatus* an enormous canopy tree, and *P. latifolius* smaller and common along upper forest margins. Two other yellowwoods occur: *P. elongatus* restricted to river banks in the south-western Cape mountains, and *P. henkelii* confined to Afromontane forests in northern Transkei and Natal.

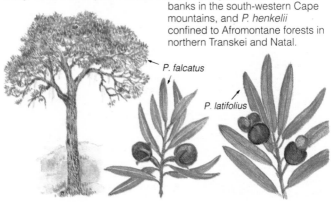

P. falcatus

P. latifolius

Diospyros mespiliformis (606)
Jackal-berry, Jakkalsbessie

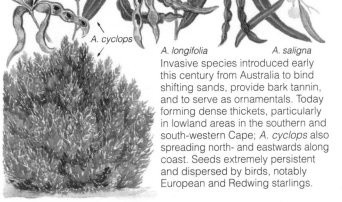

Usually a medium to large, spreading tree up to 25 m, occurring in woodlands and riverine fringes at low altitudes, often on termitaria. Bark dark grey to black and rough with deep longitudinal furrows; leaves glossy dark green above, paler below. Flowers not conspicuous; fruit edible, ripening in winter.

Acacia spp. * *A. cyclops* Red eye, Rooikrans;
* *A. longifolia* Long-leaved acacia, Gouewattel;
* *A. saligna* Port Jackson willow, Goudwilger

A. cyclops

A. longifolia   *A. saligna*

Invasive species introduced early this century from Australia to bind shifting sands, provide bark tannin, and to serve as ornamentals. Today forming dense thickets, particularly in lowland areas in the southern and south-western Cape; *A. cyclops* also spreading north- and eastwards along coast. Seeds extremely persistent and dispersed by birds, notably European and Redwing starlings.

Bridelia micrantha (324)
Mitzeerie, Mitserie

Medium to large trees up to 20 m, occurring in riverine forest, woodlands or swamp forest. Trees partly to wholly deciduous with dark glossy leaves; young foliage bronze.

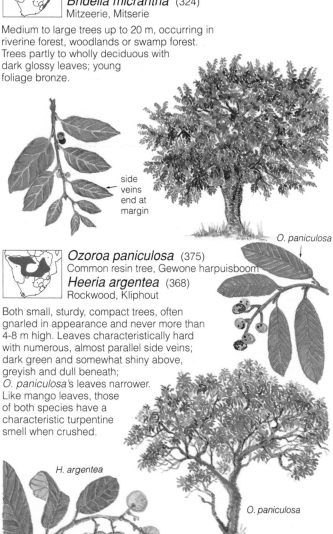

side veins end at margin

O. paniculosa

Ozoroa paniculosa (375)
Common resin tree, Gewone harpuisboom
Heeria argentea (368)
Rockwood, Kliphout

Both small, sturdy, compact trees, often gnarled in appearance and never more than 4-8 m high. Leaves characteristically hard with numerous, almost parallel side veins; dark green and somewhat shiny above, greyish and dull beneath; *O. paniculosa*'s leaves narrower. Like mango leaves, those of both species have a characteristic turpentine smell when crushed.

H. argentea

O. paniculosa

Cyphostemma spp. _C. bainesii_ Gouty vine;
C. currorii (456) Cobas, Kobas; _C. juttae_ (456,1)
Bastard cobas, Basterkobas

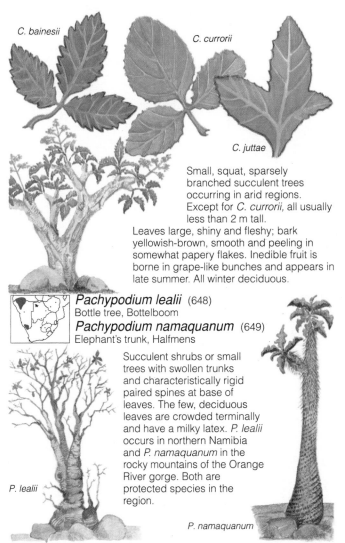

C. bainesii

C. currorii

C. juttae

Small, squat, sparsely
branched succulent trees
occurring in arid regions.
Except for _C. currorii,_ all usually
less than 2 m tall.
Leaves large, shiny and fleshy; bark
yellowish-brown, smooth and peeling in
somewhat papery flakes. Inedible fruit is
borne in grape-like bunches and appears in
late summer. All winter deciduous.

Pachypodium lealii (648)
Bottle tree, Bottelboom
Pachypodium namaquanum (649)
Elephant's trunk, Halfmens

Succulent shrubs or small
trees with swollen trunks
and characteristically rigid
paired spines at base of
leaves. The few, deciduous
leaves are crowded terminally
and have a milky latex. _P. lealii_
occurs in northern Namibia
and _P. namaquanum_ in the
rocky mountains of the Orange
River gorge. Both are
protected species in the
region.

P. lealii

P. namaquanum

Barringtonia racemosa (524)
Powder-puff tree,
Poeierkwasboom

Typically grows in dense, fringing stands along lagoon banks. Usually a small tree up to 10 m high with a compact, dark green canopy. Flowers attractive whitish-pink.

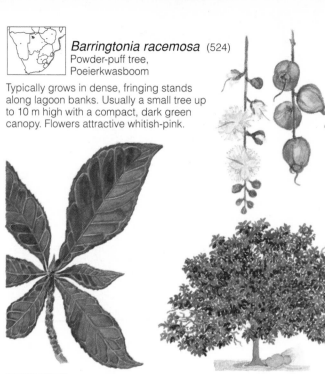

* *Salix babylonica*
Weeping willow, Huilwilgeboom

A naturalized tree, often planted along highland water courses. Grows easily from baton-sized cuttings; said to be spreading naturally.

pendulous leaves and branches

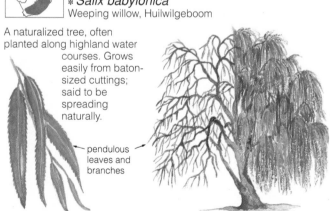

Brachylaena rotundata (730)
Mountain silver oak, Bergvaalbos
Brachylaena discolor (724 & 731)
Wild silver oak, Wildevaalbos

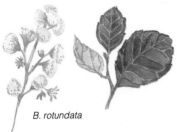

Generally small trees occurring in coastal areas (*B. discolor*) or in rocky outcrops (*B. rotundata*). Characteristic of the genus are the stiff leathery leaves – darkish green and shiny above, and dull and whitish below; leaf serrations end in soft tooth-like projections. Bark of twigs usually blackish and wrinkled.

B. rotundata

B. discolor

Leucospermum conocarpodendron (84)
Tree pincushion, Kreupelhout

A round shrub from 3-5 m high, usually found in groves. Bark thick and horizontally fissured; young twigs hairy. Leaves leathery with yellowish glands at apex of serrations. Flowers August to January.

toothed apex

Celtis africana (39)
White stinkwood, Witstinkhout
Trema orientalis (42)
Pigeonwood, Hophout

Medium to large trees found in coastal and inland forest. Leaves thin, conspicuously three-veined from base, and with rather stiff hairs making them mildly abrasive to the touch.

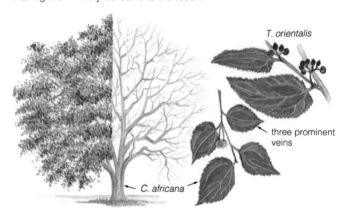

T. orientalis

three prominent veins

C. africana

Ziziphus mucronata (447)
Buffalo-thorn, Blinkblaar-wag-'n-bietjie

Common and widespread, small to medium-sized, and even extremely large trees, usually 3-6 m but up to 20 m high. Leaves fairly shiny; paired spines at base of leafstalk, one forward and one recurved, are diagnostic. Flowers inconspicuous; fruit, ripening in autumn and winter, is edible and has been used as coffee beans. Plant favoured by browsing animals.

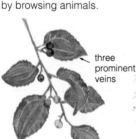

three prominent veins

Ficus sur (50)
Cape fig, Kaapse vy

Can be an extremely large, spreading tree up to 20 m or more, often occurring in forest or riverine locations. Bark grey and fairly smooth. Young leaves conspicuously pinkish-orange, maturing to green or grey-green; milky latex exuding when leaf is broken off. Heavy, branched bunches of figs on lower branches are characteristic in spring and summer.

Spirostachys africana (341)
Tamboti, Tambotie

A small tree up to 10 m with a blackish trunk; often found growing in valleys and along seasonal river courses. Bark rough with longitudinal fissures and deep horizontal cracks. Milky latex extremely toxic; even smoke from burning twigs is poisonous.

toxic latex can burn skin; smoke from burning twigs also poisonous

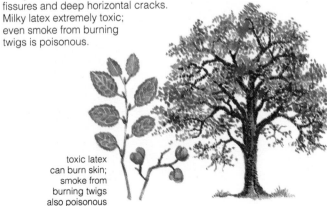

FAMILIES MORACEAE AND EUPHORBIACEAE   17

Hibiscus tiliaceus (464)
Coast hibiscus, Wildekatoenboom

A tangled, fairly stout shrub or small tree up to 8 m, occurring as a fringing 'hedge' to lagoons and tidal rivers. Leaves large, wider than they are long and with soft hairs on upper and lower surfaces. Large, showy flowers produced through spring to autumn, open butter-yellow but turn orange and even pink with age.

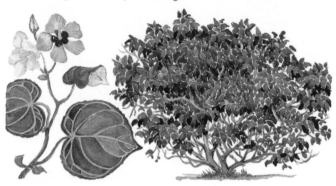

* *Populus canescens*
Grey poplar, Vaalpopulier

Originally introduced from Asia, this species usually occurs in groves but is now spreading to wetlands. Vigorous root suckers make elimination of this tree difficult.

grey below

whitish

Dombeya rotundifolia (471)
Wild pear, Gewone drolpeer

A small, neatly rounded tree up to 5 m; individual plants usually found scattered on rocky hillsides. Bark dark brown with deep, longitudinal fissures; leaves abrasive to the touch. White flowers may cover the plants in spring. Other species of *Dombeya* similar, all with three or five prominent veins extending from leaf base.

Greyia sutherlandii (446)
Natal bottlebrush, Natalse baakhout

A small tree found on open mountain-sides, often on rocky slopes. Leaves light green; inflorescences bright orange, appearing in spring. Two closely allied species *G. radlkoferi* (Transvaal bottlebrush, Transvaalse baakhout: 445), distinguished by the whitish undersides of the leaves, and *G. flanaganii* (Kei bottlebrush, Keibaakhout: 444) occur in the north and south respectively.

Combretum apiculatum (532)
Red bushwillow, Rooibos

twisted leaf-tip

Combretum hereroense (538)
Russet bushwillow, Kierieklapper

velvety beneath

Combretum imberbe (539)
Leadwood, Hardekool

greyish

vertically fissured

Combretum erythrophyllum (536)
River bushwillow,
Riviervaderlandswilg

leaves with velvety
under-surface

Combretum molle (537)
Velvet bushwillow,
Basterrooibos

medium-sized tree found in
bushveld and on open hillsides

leaves with
dense grey
velvety hairs,
especially below

Combretum zeyheri (546)
Large-fruited bushwillow,
Raasblaar

large fruit

Euclea divinorum (595)
Magic guarri, Towerghwarrie
Euclea pseudebenus (598)
Ebony tree, Ebbeboom

E. divinorum: a multi-stemmed shrub or small tree, up to 8 m but usually from 3-5 m. Occurs in lowland areas in seasonally waterlogged sites; often in dense stands with poor grass cover.

E. divinorum

E. pseudebenus: small, up to 10 m with characteristically drooping branches. Occurs in arid areas, often in seasonal stream beds where few other trees survive. Leaves very narrow and slightly curved; twigs finely hairy. Flowers inconspicuous; fruits solitary, ripening to black in late summer.

E. pseudebenus

Salvadora persica (622)
Mustard tree,
Regte mosterdboom

Mostly a small, scrambling, trailing bush 3-5 m high, occurring in arid areas along water courses. Leaves dark green and somewhat fleshy. Another species *S. angustifolia* (Transvaal mustard tree, Transvaalse mosterdboom: 621) has greyish-green leaves and occurs in the north-east.

Olea europaea (617)
Wild olive, Swartolienhout

A small to medium-sized tree usually 3-7 m high but up to 15 m, widespread in many habitats. Leaves up to 10 cm long, dull olive-green above, lightish brown below.

Terminalia prunioides (550)
Purple-pod terminalia, Sterkbos

T. prunioides has spine-tipped branchlets and occurs in bushveld on rocky hillsides and in alluvial soils. *T. sericea*, with silvery, silky haired leaves, is found in sandy soils.

Terminalia sericea (551)
Silver terminalia, Vaalboom

leaves terminally clustered

Breonadia salicina (684)
Matumi, Mingerhout

riverine tree

rough, dark bark

Rauvolfia caffra (647)
Quinine tree, Kinaboom

May be a small to large tree up to 25 m; almost always associated with water. Trunk conspicuously light brown and smooth with corky, pustulate surface. Leaves shiny, light green. Small whitish flowers appear in terminal clusters in winter and spring; fruits ripening to black. Plant with milky latex.

Halleria lucida (670)
Tree-fuchsia, Notsung

A shrub, small tree and in forest locations occasionally even a large tree, occurring in rocky areas from the coast to the Karoo. Bark grey with conspicuous vertical fissures.

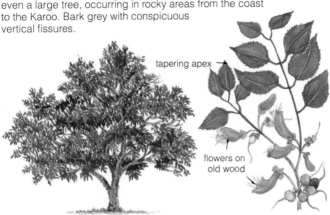

tapering apex

flowers on old wood

Buddleja salviifolia (637)
Sagewood, Wildesalie
Buddleja saligna (636)
False olive, Witolienhout

Shrubs or small trees up to 8 m, occurring on mountain-sides and upland forest margins (*B. salviifolia*), and in bushveld (*B. saligna*). Both with attractive flowers.

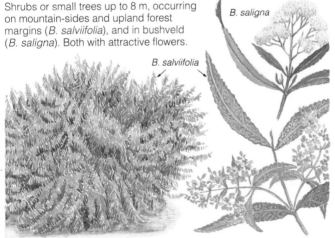

B. saligna

B. salviifolia

Diplorhynchus condylocarpon (643)
Horn-pod tree, Horingpeultjieboom

A small tree found on rocky hillsides and
in open woodland. Leaves yellowish-
green, rather shiny and tending
to droop.

Strychnos spinosa (629)
Spiny monkey orange, Groenklapper
Strychnos madagascariensis (626)
Black monkey orange, Swartklapper

Small trees with shiny leaves, though in forest
locations *S. madagascariensis* may be
a large tree. *S. spinosa* has hooked
spines on twigs.

S. madagascariensis

← *S. spinosa*

S. spinosa

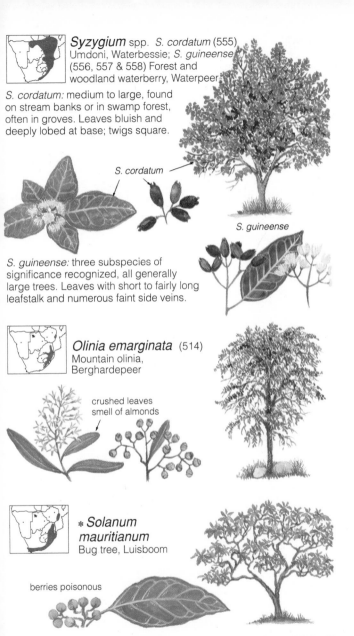

Syzygium spp. *S. cordatum* (555) Umdoni, Waterbessie; *S. guineense* (556, 557 & 558) Forest and woodland waterberry, Waterpeer;

S. cordatum: medium to large, found on stream banks or in swamp forest, often in groves. Leaves bluish and deeply lobed at base; twigs square.

S. cordatum

S. guineense

S. guineense: three subspecies of significance recognized, all generally large trees. Leaves with short to fairly long leafstalk and numerous faint side veins.

Olinia emarginata (514) Mountain olinia, Berghardepeer

crushed leaves smell of almonds

* *Solanum mauritianum* Bug tree, Luisboom

berries poisonous

* _Pinus_ spp.   _P. pinaster_ Cluster pine, Trosden;
P. patula Patula pine, Treurden;
P. halepensis Aleppo pine,
Aleppoden

P. pinaster an aggressive invader
from the Mediterranean. Small to
medium-sized, found on quartzite
mountain-sides often in clumps
or as scattered individuals.
Other common invasive pine
species in the south and south-
western Cape are _P. radiata_
(Montery pine from eastern North
America) and _P. canariensis_ (Canary
pine from the Canary Islands).

P. pinaster

P. patula introduced from
central Mexico. A medium
to large tree up to 15 m.
Particularly invasive in
upland sites in the summer
rainfall area. Needles
pendulous giving the tree a
characteristic appearance.

P. patula

P. halepensis introduced from
the central Mediterranean
basin. A small tree usually less
than 10 m and often branching
low down. Needles short and
carried in pairs but foliage
generally sparse. Commonly
planted along the roadsides
and in the towns of the Karoo;
also weakly invasive on drier
mountain-sides, particularly
those in the Cape Peninsula.

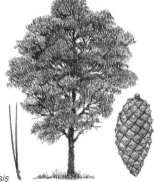

P. halepensis

Boscia foetida (124, 124,1, 127)
Smelly shepherd's tree, Stinkwitgat
Boscia albitrunca (122)
Shepherd's tree, Witgat

Usually well-shaped trees, 3-5 m high and found in arid, rocky areas. Bark of *B. albitrunca* white to whitish-grey; *B. foetida* with brown bark.

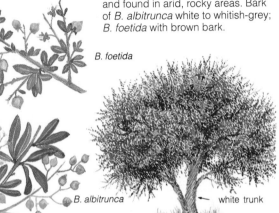

B. foetida

B. albitrunca ← white trunk

Maytenus heterophylla (399)
Common spike-thorn, Gewone pendoring
Maytenus senegalensis (402)
Confetti tree, Bloupendoring

Untidy shrubs or small trees, 3-4 m high with spine-tipped branches. *M. senegalensis* has more regularly shaped leaves.

M. senegalensis

M. heterophylla

Commiphora spp. *C. harveyi* (277) Bronze paper commiphora, Rooistamkanniedood; *C. africana* (270) Poison-grub commiphora, Harige kanniedood; *C. glaucescens* (276) Blue-leaved commiphora, Bloublaarkanniedood; *C. neglecta* (283) Sweet-root commiphora, Soetwortelkanniedood; *C. pyracanthoides* (285) Common commiphora, Gewone kanniedood

The genus comprises mostly small trees or shrubs, often found in small groves in arid areas. Most have very smooth bark with papery exfoliations. The fragrant resins are well-known sources of incense.

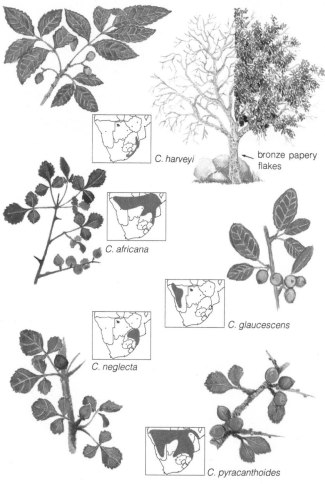

C. harveyi

← bronze papery flakes

C. africana

C. glaucescens

C. neglecta

C. pyracanthoides

Bauhinia galpinii (208,2)
Pride-of-De Kaap, Vlam-van-die-vlakte

A straggling bush, sometimes climbing and sometimes forming a small tree. Leaves characteristically two-lobed with conspicuous veins below.

Colophospermum mopane (198)
Mopane, Mopanie

A medium to large tree, usually in pure stands; can cover extensive areas and may form dense thickets as a shrub in alluvium or other poorly drained soils. Leaves drooping. An important fodder plant.

Adansonia digitata (467)
Baobab, Kremetartboom

A medium to large tree up to 25 m high, with an enormous thick trunk. Occurs at low altitudes in hot, dry bushveld.

dark grey
to coppery

Kirkia wilmsii (269)
Mountain syringa, Bergsering

A medium-sized tree found on rocky hills in the lowveld. Bark grey and smooth. Leaves crowded at ends of branches, and displaying remarkable autumn colours.

Erythrina spp. *E. caffra* (242)
Coast erythrina, Kuskoraalboom
E. lysistemon (245) Common
coral tree, Gewone koraalboom

Small to medium-sized (*E. lysistemon*)
and even large trees (*E. caffra*). Bark
light brown and smooth.
Flowers ranging from pink
to bright red.

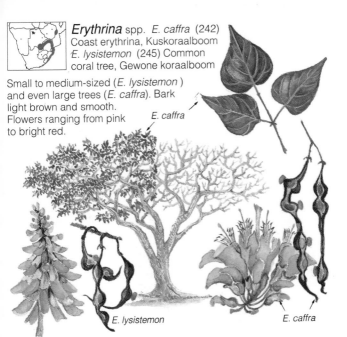

E. caffra

E. lysistemon

E. caffra

Rhus lancea (386)
Karree, Karee
Rhus undulata (395)
Kuni-bush, Koeniebos

The genus *Rhus* comprises many species from shrubs and climbers
to large trees. Species well-adapted to a wide range of conditions.

R. lancea

blunt leaftip

R. undulata

Afzelia quanzensis (207)
Pod mahogany, Peulmahonie

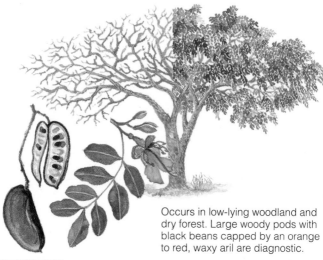

Occurs in low-lying woodland and dry forest. Large woody pods with black beans capped by an orange to red, waxy aril are diagnostic.

Schotia brachypetala (202)
Weeping boer-bean, Huilboerboon

Often a large tree with a rounded crown, occurring in open woodland and scrub forest.

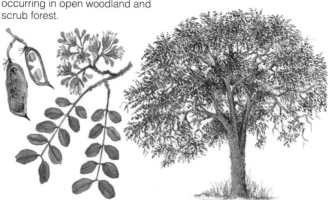

Brachystegia spiciformis
Msasa
Brachystegia boehmii
Mufuti

Medium to large trees
found in woodlands
in Zimbabwe. All
species display
spectacular
autumn colours.
Does not occur in
South Africa.

B. boehmii

B. spiciformis

Pterocarpus angolensis (236)
Transvaal teak, Kiaat

A medium to large tree with a blackish trunk having deep, vertical
fissures. Distinctive single-winged pods with bristle-covered seed
capsules are characteristic. The other three species in the region
have smooth flattened pods.

Calpurnia aurea (219 & 220)
Wild laburnum, Wildegeelkeur

A shrub or small tree with two recognized subspecies; occurs in forest, forest margins and in mesic bushveld. The small, closely allied *C. robinioides* is found mainly in the Orange Free State. Both produce attractive pendulous bunches of yellow flowers in summer and autumn, and are often grown as ornamentals.

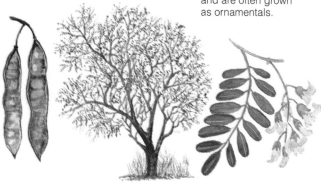

Leucosidea sericea (145)
Oldwood, Ouhout

A green or greyish-green shrub or small stout tree occurring at high altitudes on mountain slopes, along streams or along upper forest margins, usually in pure stands; sometimes in rocky river valleys. Bark reddish-brown, typically flaking off in strips; young branches shaggy due to persistent hairy stipules.

side veins end at margin

Clausena anisata (265)
Horsewood, Perdepis

A small, widespread tree usually 3-5 m, found in mesic bushveld and forests. Crushed leaves have a strong and unpleasant smell; basal leaflets conspicuously smaller than apical leaflets. Attractive white or yellow flowers appear in spring.

Zanthoxylum capense (253)
Small knobwood, Kleinperdepram

Usually a small mesic bushveld or forest tree 4-7 m, rarely reaching 15 m. Characteristic straight prickles separate this from another common species *Z. davyi* (Knobwood, Perdepram: 254), which has recurved prickles and may be a large forest tree.

crushed leaves
smell of
citrus oil

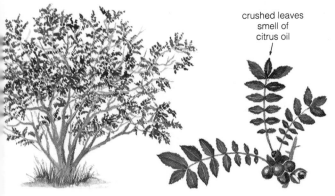

Cunonia capensis (140)
Red alder, Rooiels

Usually a large forest tree up to 30 m or more;
also common along mountain streams in the
southern and south-western Cape.
Characterized by opposite leaves
and paddle-like stipular
appendages. White to
creamy flowers grow
on long spikes at
end of branches.

Virgilia oroboides (221)
Virgilia divaricata (221,1)
Blossom tree, Keurboom

Very similar-looking trees, widely
cultivated, serving to obscure their
natural distributions. Both
are forest scrub and forest
margin species, fast
growing, with
attractive grey-
green foliage
and pink
flowers in
spring and
summer.

Lonchocarpus capassa (238)
Apple-leaf, Appelblaar

A medium to large tree found in heavy
clay soils at medium and low altitudes.
Grey-green leaves abrasive.

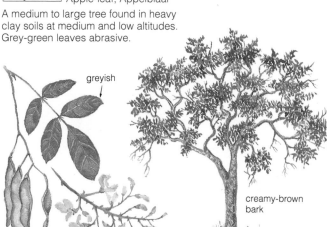

greyish

creamy-brown
bark

Trichilia dregeana (300)
Forest Natal mahogany, Bosrooiessenhout

rounded canopy

glossy, dark green above

Kigelia africana (678)
Sausage tree, Worsboom

persistent 'sausages' hang from tree

Sclerocarya birrea (360)
Marula, Maroela

A widespread, large spreading tree with fleshy, richly scented, edible fruit. Bark fairly rough, flaking in patches; leaves dark green above, paler below. Probably the most economically important bushveld tree in the region.

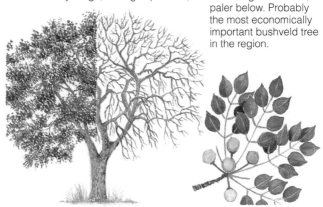

Bolusanthus speciosus (222)
Tree wistaria, Vanwykshout

A medium-sized tree with somewhat pendulous branches, occurring in bushveld at medium to low altitudes. Purple flower sprays often spectacular in spring before fresh green foliage opens.

Peltophorum africanum (215)
Weeping wattle, Huilboom

A medium-sized bushveld tree with showy, bright yellow flowers appearing in summer. Flat dark brown pods often hang in dense clusters from ends of branches.

Albizia anthelmintica (150)
Worm-cure albizia, Wurmbasvalsdoring

At most, a small untidy tree with occasional, short, sharply pointed and spine-tipped branches. Occurs in a wide variety of habitats.

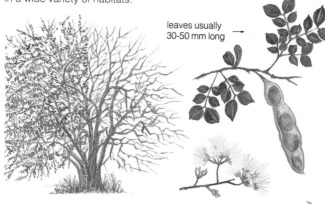

leaves usually 30-50 mm long →

Albizia adianthifolia (148)
Flat-crown, Platkroon

Can be a large tree, occurring in forest, scrub forest and in mesic woodlands. Characterized by its flat crown. Flowers reddish, often giving the canopy a pinkish tinge.

Dichrostachys cinerea (190)
Sickle bush, Sekelbos

A widespread shrub or small tree up to 6 m high, often locally common in bushveld and open savanna; also common as a scrub encroachment species. Characterized by spine-tipped branches, clusters of pods, and Chinese-lantern-type flowers in late spring and summer; plant generally multi-stemmed.

* *Prosopis glandulosa*
Mesquite, Suidwesdoring

A small naturalized tree introduced for fodder from south-western North America; now an aggressive alien in the northern Cape and large parts of Namibia. An important shade tree in arid areas; often confused with some indigenous acacias because of its strong paired spines.

Acacia albida (159)
Ana tree, Anaboom

Usually a large spreading tree typical of dry river courses and flood plains. Orange to reddish-brown pods resembling large apple peelings are characteristic.

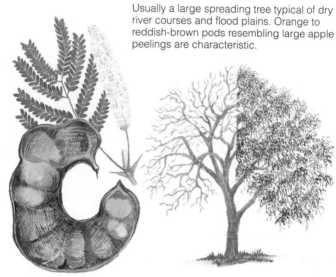

Acacia erioloba (168)
Camel thorn, Kameeldoring

A large evergreen tree with spreading branches, found in arid woodlands and along dry river beds.

Acacia tortilis (188)
Umbrella thorn,
Haak-en-steek

typical flat crown

two kinds of spines, variously arranged

Acacia xanthophloea (189)
Fever tree,
Koorsboom

yellow bark

Acacia hebeclada (170)
Candle acacia,
Trassiedoring

upright,
candle-like pods

FAMILY FABACEAE 45

Acacia haematoxylon (169)
Grey camel thorn,
Vaalkameeldoring

A small grey tree found in desert and
semi-desert areas, usually in red
sandy soils. Leaflets extremely
small, tightly packed and
overlapping, probably
to limit transpiration
loss. Bark grey-brown;
twigs densely velvety;
spines straight and
slender, and pods
long and slender.

Acacia karroo (172)
Sweet thorn,
Soetdoring

Acacia nigrescens (178)
Knob-thorn,
Knoppiesdoring

woodland and
bushveld tree

trunk with
characteristic
spine-tipped knobs

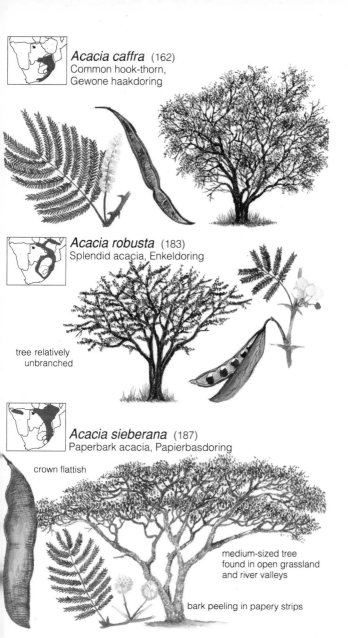

Acacia caffra (162)
Common hook-thorn,
Gewone haakdoring

Acacia robusta (183)
Splendid acacia, Enkeldoring

tree relatively
unbranched

Acacia sieberana (187)
Paperbark acacia, Papierbasdoring

crown flattish

medium-sized tree
found in open grassland
and river valleys

bark peeling in papery strips

* *Acacia mearnsii*
Black wattle, Swartwattel

A widely grown plantation species introduced from Australia for the tan-bark industry. Now an aggressive alien over all of its range, growing in dense stands along river valleys and in mountainous areas. Trees spineless, foliage dark green, and bark black and somewhat stringy.

* *Acacia dealbata*
Silver wattle, Silwerwattel

Similar to *A. mearnsii* but with a more silvery foliage and generally occurring at higher altitudes. Not widely planted, but growing in dense stands in many mountainous areas where it has become established at the expense of much of the indigenous vegetation.

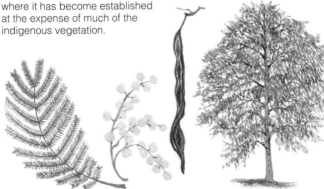

* *Jacaranda mimosifolia*
Jacaranda, Jakaranda

Introduced from the Andes, South America, this common ornamental tree has almost become South Africa's national tree. Now spreading aggressively in moist bushveld in the eastern Transvaal and northern Natal, so menacing many local species. Trees reach about 12 m in height and are characterized by clusters of bluish-mauve flowers in spring. Widely used for street planting.

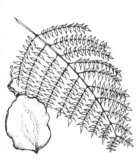

* *Melia azedarach*
Syringa, Maksering

A medium to large, east Asian, forest margin tree, widely cultivated as it is very hardy, grows quickly and provides summer shade and winter sun. Now a hostile invader, particularly in lowland areas along river banks. Syringa fruits are toxic to humans.

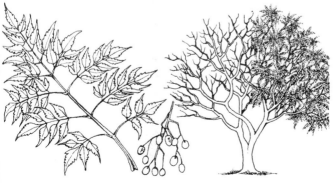

Cussonia spicata (564)
Cabbage tree, Gewone kiepersol

There are some 10 species of cabbage trees in the region. All are relatively unbranched with pale, soft, thick, corky bark. *C. spicata* is stout with a thick stem, up to 10 m high, and occurs on mountain-sides and in the dry lowveld.

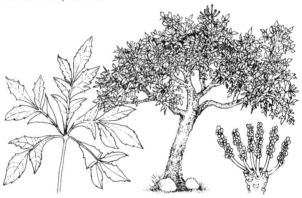

Strelitzia nicolai (34)
Natal strelitzia, Natalse wildepiesang

A multi-stemmed, banana-like tree found in coastal areas and in the Zimbabwean Highlands; mostly in rocky ravines and lowland forest where it may reach up to 15 m. Tall specimens have naked stems. Commonest of the three species found in the region; the two other species *S. alba* (White strelitzia, Kaapse wildepiesang: 32) and *S. caudata* (Transvaal strelitzia, Transvaalse wildepiesang: 33) occur in the Knysna region and along the Transvaal Drakensberg respectively.

Hyphaene coriacea (23)
Ilala palm, Lalapalm

Two *Hyphaene* species occur in the region, commonly in lowland areas on sermitaria or in low-lying, high water-table areas as a 'palm-veld'. *H. coriacea*, found in the east, is generally multi-stemmed and less than 10 m tall. Plants are often tapped for their sap which is fermented to make palm wine. *H. petersiana* (Real fan palm, Opregte waaierpalm: 24) occurs from northern Namibia eastwards to the Zambezi River and usually attains a stature of more than 15 m. Both species have hard fruits which yield 'vegetable ivory' when the husk is removed. One other fan-leaved palm found in the region in eastern Zimbabwe and Mozambique is *Borassus aethiopum* (Borassus palm, Borassuspalm: 25), which can reach 20 m or more.

Phoenix reclinata (22)
Wild date palm, Wildedadelboom

Generally a multi-stemmed reclining palm, widespread, particularly in low-lying areas and along river courses. Plants are usually less than 5 m high but may be up to 10 m.

In north-eastern Natal and southern Mozambique sap is extracted from the flower-stalk and used in the production of wine. Fruit resembles the commercial date but is smaller and less fleshy. A superficially similar palm *Jubaeopsis caffra* (Pondo coconut, Pondokokospalm: 27) occurs only in Pondoland in the Mtentu and Msikaba river valleys.

Aloe arborescens (28,1)
Krantz aloe, Kransaalwyn

Possibly the most widespread and variable of all the aloes, occurring in diverse habitats usually in rocky areas; most conspicuous at medium altitudes along forest margins. Branches into many stems but rarely reaches more than 3 m high.

Aloe bainesii (28)
Tree aloe, Boomaalwyn

Largest of the region's aloes up to 18 m tall, and in fact our only true tree aloe. Naturally grows in dense bush, forested ravines and on rugged hillsides, but has been widely planted by local people who believe it protects the homestead from lightning. Today most commonly seen marking old kraal sites, and in gardens in the country. Characterized by bare stems and narrow, dull green leaves which pale towards the margins.

Aloe dichotoma (29)
Quiver tree, Kokerboom

This and the superficially similar *A. pillansii* (Bastard quiver tree, Basterkokerboom: 30) occur in the arid western parts of the northern Cape and southern Namibia. Both have smooth papery stems, but *A. dichotoma* is much more densely branched and generally stouter. In the past the San made quivers from the bark of smaller branches.

Aloe ferox (29,2)
Bitter aloe, Bitteraalwyn

A widespread and locally common species producing intensely red inflorescences in winter, often covering valleys and hillslopes in colour. Characteristically, stems are densely sheathed with persistent old dried leaves – today stripped for commercial use, so exposing fire-sensitive stems to grass fires. A closely allied species *A. candelabrum* occurs in Natal, and is distinguished from *A. ferox* by its longer, more reflexed leaves.

Aloe pluridens (30,1)
French aloe, Fransaalwyn

This aloe occurs in forest scrub and can be more than 6 m high. Lower stem typically bare but upper-third clothed in persistent old leaves. Pink flowers appear in late autumn and early winter. Two similar-looking species *A. rupestris* (Bottlebrush aloe, Borselaalwyn: 30,3) and *A. angelica* (Wylliespoort aloe, Wylliespoortaalwyn: 28,4) occur in Natal's coastal bush and the Soutpansberg respectively. All lack persistent leaves at base, as none grows in fire-prone vegetation and so do not require insulation.

Aloe marlothii (29,5)
Flat-flowered aloe, Bergaalwyn

Locally common in bushveld, this spiny-leaved aloe produces bright yellow and orange to red flowers in winter. Extremely large specimens more than 10 m tall have been recorded which, clothed in persistent dried leaves, are a majestic sight. Flower spikes are borne horizontally rather than vertically. A similar-looking species *A. spectabilis* (Natal aloe, Natalaalwyn: 30,6) produces more upright inflorescences and occurs to the south in the Tugela Basin.

Euphorbia cooperi (346)
Lesser candelabra tree,
Transvaalse kandelaarnaboom

A spiny, succulent tree up to 10 m,
occurring on rocky outcrops in scrub and
wooded areas, usually in localized clumps.
Trunk usually naked and topped by a bush
of recurved branches – deeply divided
into deltoid shaped, four- to six-winged
segments. All succulent euphorbias
contain milky latex, exuding if the plant is
damaged or cut; this is extremely toxic and
can cause blindness and in some cases
can burn the skin. The latex of *E. cooperi*,
considered one of the most poisonous of
the *Euphorbia* species, has a typically
pungent smell.

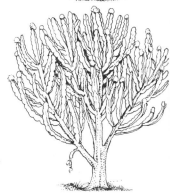

Euphorbia grandidens (350)
Large-toothed euphorbia,
Groottandnaboom

At almost 20 m possibly the tallest
of our euphorbias. Usually grows in
groves in dry forest sites and in steep,
north-facing river valleys. Often has
a number of main upright branches,
topped by bunches of green branches
which may be flattened to three-
angled. Branch margins wavy and
with small scattered paired spines.

Euphorbia ingens (351)
Candelabra tree,
Gewone naboom

Most spectacular, widespread
and probably best known of the
region's euphorbias. A massively
branched tree up to 10 m or more,
occurring as scattered individuals
or in localized concentrations
in arid bushveld. Young plants
extremely frost sensitive, thus their
incidence is a good indicator of
a frost-free area.

Euphorbia tetragona (354)
Honey euphorbia,
Heuningnaboom

A robust, spiny euphorbia occurring in dry river valleys. Usually with a single stem, dividing into several sturdy stems near the ground and topped by bushy, four- or five-angled branchlets. Flowers produce plentiful nectar which, like other euphorbia nectar, has an unpleasant flavour and can burn the mouth and throat severely. Surprisingly the latex is used in Transkei to dull toothache.

Euphorbia tirucalli (355)
Rubber hedge euphorbia,
Kraalnaboom

A widely cultivated hedge plant, thus with an enhanced distribution which obscures its natural range; commonly grows in groves. Trees usually well-branched. Small (10-20 mm) strap-like leaves produced on young branches in summer may persist for a few months if good rains occur. The only tree euphorbia species not having angular stems.

Euphorbia triangularis (356)
River euphorbia, Riviernaboom

A tall species up to 16 m or more, locally abundant on steep dry slopes in valley bushveld. Rounded main stem may develop two or more side stems. Not always easily distinguished from E. tetragona as it is relatively unbranched and also topped by small branches – generally three-angled but may be four- or five-angled. Many of the tree-like euphorbias are difficult to recognize and one is advised to consult a specialist for certain identification.

Ecological considerations

The map on the inside front cover depicts the various broad ecological regions (biomes) of southern Africa. Each of these regions has its own characteristic flora, and the tree constituent is no exception.

The region where trees are scarcest is the desert biome. Here, the only trees found are along drainage lines or on rocky outcrops where run-off from what little rainfall there is accumulates. Where they occur, trees are scattered individually and are typically of a low stature, deciduous and often succulent.

The succulent and nama karoo regions are not much richer in tree flora but, because rainfall is higher here, there are more individuals in suitable localities. Also, more evergreen species occur, especially in succulent karoo where the rainfall reliability index is fairly high.

Trees are also rare in the fynbos biome of the south and south-western Cape. This biome is characterized by the presence, and usually dominance, of dwarf shrubs and bushes; actual woody plants of any real stature are relatively scarce. Part of the reason for this is that frequent fires maintain a low vegetation cover, meaning that the only trees that occur are those on rocky outcrops, in ravines and in infrequently burned veld. Even where there are trees, these are short, 3-5 m at most, and those that are able to survive fires are equipped with a thick bark for protection.

The grassland biome is also by definition relatively free of trees. This is perhaps because the grassland regions of southern Africa, including the Highveld and the area around Harare, are old landscapes. It would seem that trees thrive on geologically recent landscapes. Old landscapes have old soils from which all the important plant nutrients have been leached, leaving behind the toxic aluminium ions which can be so concentrated as to prevent plant growth. Trees that do occur in grassveld are usually found in valleys and on rocky hillslopes.

Where trees are a feature is in the savanna and forest biomes. Both evergreen and deciduous species are typical of open arid savanna, the former in the nutrient-poor soils (mainly Kalahari sands) and the latter in the richer loams and clays. The moist savannas are characterized by fairly low, dense tree communities in South Africa, but in Zimbabwe the trees tend to be tall with straight, relatively unbranched trunks, forming the characteristic 'miombo' region.

The forests of the region have mainly Afromontane links, many of the families, genera and even species having a wide distribution in Africa. The cool subtropical forests are characterized by evergreen species, festooned with epiphytic lichens, mosses, ferns and orchids, while in the more tropical forests, a denser woody component forms the understorey which is much richer in species. Along the east coast a specialized dune forest community with a low dense canopy occurs; this is generally rich in woody climbers which lace the canopies together and tend to seal the understorey from wind. Swamp forests, usually poor in species but rich in productivity, occur in wet lowland sites. Because their soils are among the best in the region, these forests are often cleared for agriculture. Finally, there are the mangrove communities which once abounded in some estuaries, but which today are severely restricted because silt, due to poor agricultural methods, has filled the estuaries; many are also polluted, and the biggest estuaries have been destroyed to build harbours.

Utilization of trees

When we think of trees it is usually thoughts of cool shade and other aspects of their beauty that come to mind; it may be of the bird and animal life they support. However, trees are among our richest and most versatile resources, and progressively are being found to be potential sources of a wide variety of products. It is well known that many trees produce edible fruits; some are sources of gum, dye, sugar or fibre, but today the most used part of trees is the wood. Apart from its obvious value in construction and as a fuel, wood is a valuable source of paper and chemicals, and already, synthetic fabrics such as rayon, rubber, plastics, packaging material and cellophane are being produced from wood.

Currently, some 12 billion tonnes of wood are utilized worldwide per annum. Wood is comprised of four basic materials: cellulose (50% or more of the bulk), hemi-cellulose (20%), lignin (25%) and resin or oils (the remainder). Since the 1940s cellulose has been converted into rayon fibre; it is used as paper and fluff for disposable nappies, and is altered chemically to form a thickening agent for paints and puddings. It is also added to washing powder to make cottons more dirt-resistant, and polyesters more wettable and easier to launder. Today industrial chemists are seeking to replace petrochemicals with cellulose compounds for use in cosmetics, lacquers, and to size fabrics.

Hemi-cellulose has long been turned into xylitol in Finland, where it is known as birch sugar and used in the manufacture of mints, throat pastilles and chewing gum. Unlike sucrose it does not cause tooth decay and is now being marketed as an alternative sweetener.

The lignin component of trees serves to strengthen and protect the plant from the ravages of climate and insect attack. This substance is in fact a natural polymer, yet millions of tonnes are dumped or burnt annually, as it is considered a waste product. Although it is difficult to break lignin down chemically, it has been successfully used in the manufacture of certain products such as vanilla flavouring; it has also been used experimentally in adhesives and as an additive to cement. Lignin may one day be a vital source of polystyrenes, plastics and dyes, replacing those currently derived from petrochemicals.

Wood is sure to be used even more extensively in future and, because it is a renewable resource, by using wood we will be able to conserve many other non-renewable resources. Thus, experts are proposing that massive tree-planting programmes be implemented worldwide so as to replenish depleted landscapes and guarantee a continuous supply for the future. This in turn will necessitate careful management and a knowledgeable public to ensure that the right trees are planted in the right places, and then wisely and purposefully used.

Gardening with trees

There are many indigenous trees which can be successfully cultivated in the ordinary suburban garden, and in southern Africa there are some 1 500 of these from which to choose. Not all species will be suited to your particular location and site, so before you decide on what to plant, make sure that local conditions (rainfall, wind, soil type, etc.) will allow for optimum growth of the tree.

Different trees offer different advantages and before choosing a species ask yourself questions like 'How big a tree do I want?' (remember size has a height and a spread component); 'How quickly do I want the tree to grow?; Do I want a deciduous tree to provide winter sun and summer shade?; Will the roots interfere with the foundations of a building, swimming pool or with the sewage system?' Decide on the foliage colour you want, and whether you would like a flowering or fruiting tree – many of these will attract fruit-eating or nectar-gathering birds, while some species may provide nesting and roosting sites. You can, with care and advice from your local nurseryman, create an area that will provide a habitat for various animal species, and so enrich and diversify your local environment.

Just as much care must be taken in preparing the ground and planting a young tree as in choosing it. Most important is to dig a proper hole: this should be square and should measure at least one cubic metre. The bigger the hole, the better the tree will grow. Examine the soil, and remember that sandy soil is very porous and will require more watering than a good loam soil. One way of overcoming the problem of porous soil is to line the bottom of the hole with plastic, so preventing the water from draining away too quickly. Clay soil, on the other hand, is not porous and so tends to retain water, becoming waterlogged and causing roots to rot. With clay soil it may be necessary to provide some sort of French drain, or to fill the first 20-25 cm of the hole with clean stones and so encourage better drainage. Regardless of the soil type, it is a good idea to place a piece of plastic pipe (3-10 cm diameter) in the hole with one end above the soil surface; this will allow you to water the roots directly, rather than relying on water to penetrate through the soil from above.

plastic pipe to facilitate watering

Before returning the soil to the planting hole, fill the bottom third of the hole with 3-4 spadefuls of compost or manure, then fill to the half-way mark with soil.

Once the tree is in position, fill in the hole with a mixture of soil, compost and manure; this will help provide essential nutrients for a young tree. If your area is subject to extreme heat, cold or wind, a piece of shade cloth or hessian tied around the tree in the first year or two will greatly assist growth.

Clubs and societies

Societies catering specifically for tree enthusiasts are:
The Tree Society of South Africa, P O Box 4416, Johannesburg 2000
The Dendrological Society, P O Box 104, Pretoria 0001

Societies catering for more general interests are:
The Botanical Society of South Africa, Kirstenbosch, Claremont 7735
The Wildlife Society of Southern Africa, P O Box 44189, Linden 2104

Further reading

Coates Palgrave, K. 1983. *Trees of Southern Africa,* Struik.
De Winter, B., Vahrmeijer, J., Von Breitenbach, F. 1978. *The National List of Trees,* Van Schaik.
Moll, E.J. 1981. *Trees of Natal,* UCT Eco-Lab Trust Fund.
Palmer, E., Pitman, N. 1972. *Trees of Southern Africa,* Balkema.
Van Wyk, P. 1974. *Trees of the Kruger National Park,* Purnell.

Glossary

Aril An appendage on a seed, usually oily or waxy and often attractive to animals.

Afromontane forests Those forests found in the tropics on cooler mountain slopes.

Biome A region of similar climate having a homogenous vegetation.

Bipinnate When a leaf is twice pinnate (*see* Pinnate).

Browser An animal that feeds on leaves, shoots and twigs.

Bushveld A savanna area with mixed trees, shrubs and grasses.

Canopy The highest level of foliage in a forest, formed by crowns of trees.

Epiphyte A plant growing on another plant and not rooted in the soil.

Exfoliations Peeling layers or flakes of bark.

Fascicled Describing leaves in tight bunches.

Leaf *see* illustrations opposite.

Latex A milky fluid produced by some plants.

Mesic Relating to moist conditions (opposite of xeric or dry).

Miombo *Brachystegia* woodland of central Africa.

Palmate When a compound leaf has its leaflets radiating outwards in the shape of a hand.

Pinnate When a compound leaf has its leaflets in two rows on either side of the stalk.

Scrub Low, dense bush – almost impenetrable.

Stipule A scale- or leaf-like outgrowth at the base of the leaf where the leafstalk joins the twig; may be modified to form spines.

Termitaria The mounds made by termites.

Trifoliolate When a leaf is divided into three segments.

Understorey The plants that grow under a tree canopy or overstorey.

A compound leaf (pinnate)

A simple leaf

Index

Numbers in **bold** indicate main species entry

Index to tree codes

How to use the key

The table opposite has been carefully designed to make tree species identification as simple, literally, as 1, 2, 3. Once you understand the three steps involved in obtaining a code, you will be able to identify the tree species appearing in this book. Identification is based solely on leaf characteristics, so it is necessary to obtain a leaf, or preferably a small twig, from the tree you want to identify before you can use the table. Remember also that only 10% of southern African tree species are represented in this guide.

The table comprises ten columns numbered from 0-9, and three rows. The columns will provide the three digits needed to form the tree code, but first you must define your leaf according to the three rows. The first row requires that you characterize your leaf and the next two that you measure the length and width. Once you have matched your leaf with one of the characteristics in each row of the table, you will obtain a three-digit code. Codes are arranged numerically on page 63 and will refer you to one or more pages on which you can match your leaf or twig and tree with one illustrated.

Before you can identify the leaf character (row 1) it is important to know a little about the different types of leaves that occur. Leaves are either simple (not divided) or compound (divided into leaflets), although some simple leaves are so deeply lobed or segmented as to appear almost compound (see *Cyphostemma juttae* p. 13). Further, leaves are variously arranged on the stem: they may be opposite (some are almost opposite, or sub-opposite), or whorled (several leaves arising from the same point), or alternate. Finally, leaf margins differ: basically these are either entire or not entire. If they are not entire, they may be serrated, coarsely toothed, scalloped or wavy.

With this knowledge you can now use the table to obtain a code. Trees with no leaves, euphorbias for instance, are simple to code (000). Note that euphorbias have also been coded according to column 9 (specialized growth forms), but both code combinations will lead you to the right species. Most trees have definable leaves which can be classified according to columns 1-8; those with specialized growth forms have been coded separately (9). Decide whether the leaf is simple (1,2,3,4 or 8) or compound (5,6 or 7). If simple, are the leaves alternately arranged (1,2 or 8) or opposite (3 or 4)? Then, look at whether the leaf margin is entire or not. You will notice that for leaves that are bunched, or fascicled (8) it does not matter whether the margins are entire or not. The code group represented by column 1 is the most complex, but has been simplified by distinguishing between trees with milky latex (*1*) (exuding from a broken twig or leaf) and those without (**1**).

As an example, say that you have the leaf of *Acacia karroo:* the leaves are bipinnately compound (7). Leaf length, measured from stem to leaftip is from 55-100 mm (6); leaf width measures 21-40 mm (6). Your code is thus 766, which refers you to pages 45 and 46: you would see that your leaf matches that of *Acacia karroo* on page 46.